"This book fills a need in the local church. Much is said about the Gospel, and Eli takes the time to unpack its profound meaning in an everyday context. I can only see good things for the study group that reads through it together."

Pastor Mike Dente
Calvary Chapel Paris
Paris, France

"Eli Taft has been a longtime friend and source of academic and biblical information for many years. The legacy that he has left in my life through his mentorship and friendship is second to none. In Gospel Roots he continues that legacy at a broader level by extending his extensive knowledge to the body of Christ. This book should be on every Christian's reading list."

Father Joshua Gilliam
Resurrection Anglican Church
Kannapolis, NC USA

"Pastor Eli has written a great book explaining the Good News of Jesus Christ. It is easy to understand. A great resource for teaching new Christians, small groups, and discipleship classes."

Pastor Keith Navey
Eva Drive Baptist Church
Concord, NC USA

Gospel Roots

Restoring a Biblical Understanding of the Good
News of Jesus Christ

Eli Taft

ISBN: 0-578-49071-4
ISBN-13: 978-0-578-49071-7

As of this writing, this book is also
available as a free PDF download:
http://www.elitaft.com/gospel-roots/

CONTENTS

CHAPTER ONE

THE GOSPEL

Introduction

In recent years there has been an increased emphasis on the gospel in many Christian churches. Pastors and teachers have been speaking out about the importance of knowing the gospel, believing the gospel, living out the gospel, and sharing the gospel. This has been a great thing.

At the same time, this beautiful resurgence has also resulted in the occasional misuse of the word to mean different things in various contexts. It has become a buzzword. It is being used in ways that have convoluted its meaning. Does "gospel" refer to a certain kind of music, church, lifestyle, mindset, or something else?

Good News

The word "gospel" simply means "good news." It is news, but not just any kind of news. It is *good* news. News that makes one glad, and it was never meant to be complicated. It is powerful in its simplistic beauty. The purpose of this book is to provide a simple and biblical understanding of the good news of Jesus Christ.

Why the Gospel?

Jesus' public ministry was described in the Bible as going from city to city, preaching the gospel and calling all men to repent and believe (Matt. 4:23, 9:35; Mark. 1:15). When Jesus called Peter and Andrew to be His disciples, He told them He would make them "fishers of men" (Matt. 4:18-19). This was not only a call to belief, but a call to action. They spent years with Jesus, listening to His teaching, observing His miracles, and being trained by Him to fulfill the calling He had given them.

When Jesus sent out the twelve apostles on a mission to proclaim the kingdom of God, they went preaching the gospel and calling all men to repent, just like Jesus had (Luke 9:1-6; Mark 6:12). He also sent out seventy disciples with a similar mission (Luke 10:1-17). These missions were part of their training, preparing them for the much larger mission that Jesus intended for them.

Jesus told them later on that the gospel would eventually be preached to the whole world (Matt. 24:14). This was a much larger scale mission than the surrounding villages they had been trained for. When Jesus rose from the dead, before His ascension, He reiterated this mission when He told them to make disciples, baptize them, and teach them to observe all that He commanded (Matt. 28:19-20). Or as Mark puts it, "Go into all the world and preach the gospel to all creation" (16:15). He told them that they were to be His witnesses, bringing the gospel to the "remotest parts of the earth" (Acts 1:8).

The apostles took this command very seriously. They shared the gospel at every opportunity. Even when tremendous persecution broke out in Jerusalem, the disciples that scattered went throughout the regions spreading the gospel everywhere they went (Acts 8:4, 11:20). From that time, all the way up to the present, disciples of Jesus Christ have been committing their lives—often with great cost, including persecution and death—to fulfilling this mission.

Why the gospel? Because the gospel is foundational to the Christian faith. Jesus preached the gospel and taught His disciples to do the same. It is by the gospel that men can be restored to God. Without the gospel, there is no hope.

> "WHOEVER WILL CALL ON THE NAME OF THE LORD WILL BE SAVED." How then will they call on Him in whom they have not believed? How will they believe in Him whom they have not heard? And how will they hear without a preacher? So faith [comes] from hearing, and hearing by the word of Christ. (Rom. 10:13-14, 17)

> But I do not consider my life of any account as dear to myself, so that I may finish my course and the ministry which I received from the Lord Jesus, to testify solemnly of the gospel of the grace of God. (Acts 20:24)

Good News…About What?

Imagine someone were to come up to you and say, "I have great news!" How would you respond? Would you simply thank them, and say you really appreciate them telling you that they have great news? Certainly not! You would want to know what the good news is, right? It's the content of the message that matters.

If the gospel means good news, the next logical question to ask is, "Good news about what?"

The Bible speaks about the gospel of the kingdom, the gospel of the grace of God, the gospel of Jesus Christ, etc. Which is it?

On the one hand, the gospel is all of these things. The good news is about the kingdom. It is about God, and about His grace, and about His Son, Jesus Christ. It is the good news that God has provided a way to restore us to Himself through the death, resurrection, and ascension of His Son, Jesus Christ. It is a wonderful, beautiful, and urgent message.

On the other hand, the gospel is not just a catch phrase to mean anything related to God or Christianity in general. It's not to be used as a buzzword to mean anything we want it to mean. It's a specific message that has specific content for a specific purpose, and it is important that we understand it. We need to know it in order to be restored to God. We also need to be reminded of it over and over again as we live as Christians in this world. Christians also need to be able to explain it to others, since we are commanded to do so:

> "Go into all the world and preach the gospel to all creation" (Mark 16:15).

Good News for Everyone

One of the greatest things about the gospel is also one of the things that makes the news so good. It's good news for *everyone*. It's not just good news for people who speak a certain language, live in a particular part of the world, have reached a specific age, have a specific social status, or anything else. It's for everyone. In the book of Acts, the apostles preached this message to a wide range of people, including Israelites, Romans, Gentiles, Ethiopians, and basically anybody that would listen. It was for "every soul" (Acts 3:23), "every nation" (Acts 10:35), and "everyone" (Acts 13:39). This pretty much sums it up:

> For the promise is for you and your children and for all who are far off, as many as the Lord our God will call to Himself (Acts 2:39).

As you go through this book, keep in mind that this isn't a history lesson. It's not just about something that happened a long time ago. It's not about something that only applies to other people. These words are truth and life, and are meant for you specifically.

Good News for Believers

The apostles continued to preach "repentance

toward God and faith in our Lord Jesus Christ" even among well-established churches (Acts 20:21). Why? Because the gospel isn't just about how to become a Christian. It continues to point us to Christ, remind us of our desperate need for Him, bring us closer to God, and empower us to be used by Him in this world. The gospel is not just for non-believers. It's for all believers.

Gospel Roots

It is important to recognize that the gospel has multiple parts. The metaphor of a tree is wonderful to demonstrate this. Trees are high and lofty and beautiful, but they are nothing without their roots. In the same way, the gospel is a message that is made up of distinct parts (or "roots") that are all necessary. If someone tells you that God loves you, they have told you the truth, but they have not told you the gospel. They have told you part of it, and all the parts matter. That's why the angel of the Lord commanded the apostles to speak the "whole message" (Acts 5:20).

In the following chapters, we will look at the foundational and essential elements of the good news. These chapters have been based on the various sermons recorded in the book of Acts. The reason is simple. Jesus was the first to preach this gospel, and the apostles learned it directly from Him. They were the first ones to preach the gospel after Jesus. We should be able to learn from their sermons what are the essential elements of the gospel message.

My hope is that this book will result in a much deeper understanding of the gospel that is powerful and life-changing, that it will ignite a fire within you to be restored to God and to love Him more than anything, and that it will enable you to explain the gospel to others in a clear and easy-to-understand way.

Reflection Questions

If you have heard the gospel before, can you remember the first time you heard it and what effect it had on you?

Do you feel like you are already familiar with the gospel? If so, how would you explain it to someone else?

Do you have any concerns or confusion about the word "gospel?" Any questions you hope will be answered in reading this book?

Do you think it's possible to believe a false gospel, and if so, can you think of any examples of what a false gospel might be?

CHAPTER TWO

GOD

Introduction

The good news starts with God because all things start with God. The very first words in the Bible are "In the beginning God" (Gen. 1:1). John begins his gospel account with "In the beginning was the Word, and the Word was with God, and the Word was God" (John 1:1). If we do not have a basic understanding of God, then we won't understand what makes the gospel good news.

> The heavens are telling of the glory of God; And their expanse is declaring the work of His hands (Ps. 19:1).

Since the creation of the world His invisible attributes, His eternal power and divine nature, have been clearly seen, being understood through what has been made, so that they are without excuse (Rom. 1:20).

Even though the Bible says we should be able to understand who God is from the evidence all around us, the Bible also says mankind rejected these revelations, and that this rejection came with an unimaginably high cost—our hearts grew dark and our minds were corrupted (Rom. 1:21-32). This is why there is such diversity in ideas about God among the nations. Even with this evidence all around us, we can't make sense of it on our own.

This chapter will look at how the apostles described God when they first began preaching the gospel in the book of Acts. The goal is to have a better understanding of Who God is, which paves the way to a better understanding of the gospel as a whole. We will look at three main attributes of God —Creator, Lord, and Father—and consider other attributes that are related these.

Creator

God is the Creator of everything. We begin with this attribute because it is the very first thing God ever chose to reveal about Himself in the

Scriptures. Genesis 1:1 reads, "In the beginning God created the heavens and the earth." When preaching the gospel to the people of Athens, Paul said that God made the "world and all things in it" (Acts 17:24). God literally made everything from nothing. Just think about some of the things this tells us about God!

Consider a painting. In some ways, a painting can be understood as an attempt by the painter to create an expression of himself. In the same way, God created everything to express something about Himself. By beginning with God as Creator, we can begin to understand certain things about Him.

Holy

If God created everything, then He existed before everything else. If that is the case, then there is truly nothing else like Him. This difference between God and everything else is so great that it is often said that God is "wholly other."

Consider the analogy of the painter again. Even though a painter uses art to express something about himself, no single painting tells you all there is to know about him. Even if you bought every painting that he ever painted, you would never know all there is to know about him. You would only know what he has chosen to reveal in his work.

A painter who paints a lot of sailboats might be expressing his love for adventure or the open sea. But this tells you nothing about other aspects of his life.

In the same way, even though we can learn a lot about God by considering what He has made, and how and why He has made it, we must begin by acknowledging that we are limited in our ability to understand Him. We can only understand Him in ways He has chosen to reveal Himself to us.

Everything in creation, including us, is only a partial expression of a God that is so great, so wholly other, that we cannot possibly comprehend the fullness of how great He is. This idea of being wholly other is another way of saying God is holy. This thought of God's holiness should spark in us an awe of how great God is, and a delight and desire to know Him more.

> "There is no one holy like the LORD, Indeed, there is no one besides You, Nor is there any rock like our God" (1 Sam. 2:2).

Eternal

If God created everything, then He existed before anything. Think about it. If anything existed before God, then He could not have created everything. This includes time. If time existed before God, and God was bound to the constraints of time, then it wouldn't be true to say that God created everything. If God truly created everything, including time, then that means He exists outside of time. He could not create time if it already existed before Him.

In other words, God is eternal. He has no beginning and no end. God spoke through Isaiah the prophet, "Before Me there was no God formed, and there will be none after Me" (43:10), and "I am the first and I am the last, and there is no God besides Me" (44:6).

You might think this is hard to imagine, but what is the alternative? What would it mean if God had a beginning? The first question we would probably ask is, "What existed before Him?" This is why God being eternal is not just an interesting idea. It's an essential category of His nature. For God to be God, He has to have existed before everything else; otherwise we would not call Him God. We could call the thing that existed before Him God.

If God exists outside of time, it means He does not experience events unfolding in the sequential way that we do. We are finite, bound to experience events as they occur along the thread of time. We can never go back to a previous time, nor can we jump ahead to see how things turn out later. The Bible says that God is not like this. For God, "one day is like a thousand years, and a thousand years is like one day" (2 Pet. 3:8). This is one of the many ways in which God is holy, or completely "other." It's hard for created beings to even understand what it must be like to have no beginning and no end. Even if we understand that it is a necessary attribute of God, it's not something that we can fully comprehend. He can see the beginning and the end as clearly as He can see the present.

Omniscient

If God created everything, then He knows everything. After all, He created it. Imagine how great the mind of God must be, that He could create not only galaxies and universes but atoms and molecules! To say God knows everything is to say that God is omniscient. He knows and sees everything. He counts and names the stars. He knows the number of hairs on your head (Luke 12:7). His "understanding is infinite" (Ps. 147:4-5).

Speaking of infinite: If God is outside of time, then He doesn't only know everything that has been. He doesn't only know everything that is.

God also knows everything that will be. One of the things that the apostles point out quite often, regarding the gospel, is that God knew what would happen. Peter said that Jesus was crucified by the "foreknowledge of God" (Acts 2:23). Nothing in the gospel story was a surprise to God. None of it caught Him off-guard. He wasn't off-duty for any of it. He hadn't over-slept. All of it was part of the plan.

God sees the end from the beginning. What a great thought! If He knows everything that will happen, then it means He has chosen to do all of the things He's done with full knowledge of what would happen next in the story. It means there's a greater picture than we realize. There is a future we have not yet entered into that God already knows perfectly, and all of it is part of His ultimate plan.

Predetermination

If God created everything, then He knows everything that is and will be, but there is more to it than that. He is not a helpless bystander with no control over how it all turns out in the end. Paul said that God has determined the "appointed times" of every man (Acts 17:26). Concerning the gospel, the apostles made it clear that God not only knew what would happen; He actually determined for it to happen. Peter said that God predetermined the death of His own Son (Acts 2:23). This is why Jesus could confidently predict His own death and resurrection (Mark 8:31).

If God only knew the future, but had no control over it, how could we be certain that He was telling the truth? How could *He* be certain of it? This is an important aspect of the gospel—the fact that the events concerning Jesus were in fulfillment of prophecies in the Old Testament. If those details couldn't be guaranteed (or "predetermined"), how could we be confident that God would predict them accurately? If God is not able to intervene and determine an outcome, His predictions would always have the potential to be mistaken. Foreknowledge without predetermination would be very unstable. It would take all of the power out of statements such as this:

> "Now I declare new things; Before they spring forth I proclaim them to you" (Isa. 42:9).

> "Now I have told you before it happens, so that when it happens, you may believe" (John 14:29).

The power of God to not only know the future, but determine it, means that God can guarantee His promises. It means we can trust Him. It means that His promises will absolutely come to pass, and nothing can deter them. This is a wonderful thing to remember when we read promises that God has given us in the Bible.

Lord

When Paul told the Athenians that God is the Creator of everything, he also told them that God was Lord. He said, "The God who made the world and all things in it, since He is Lord of heaven and earth" (Acts 17:24). God is Creator, and He is also Lord. Is this distinction useful? Can't it just be assumed that God is Lord over everything because He created it? Could God create everything and not be Lord of it?

Technically, He could. The difference between being Creator and being Lord is that creation refers to what God has done and Lordship refers to what God is doing. It has to do with His on-going relationship with His creation. God did not simply create everything, set it all in motion like a child's spinner toy, and turn to play with something else while it spins slowly to a stop and eventually topples over. He's not distant, disinterested, or absent. He didn't walk away. He is—and has always been, and will always be—Lord of all.

Omnipotent

If God is Lord of everything, He is more powerful than anything. If anything were more powerful than Him, it could not be said that He is Lord of all. In other words, God is omnipotent, or all-powerful.

Imagine if this were not the case. If God was not all-powerful, no plan of His could be guaranteed. No promise of His could be trusted. Why would anyone pray to God if there were things outside of His control? How could we trust that our prayers would make any difference? If we end up getting what we've prayed for, how could we be certain whether God had answered our prayer? If God were not omnipotent, the answer to our prayer might just as well have been nothing more than an anomaly—some random factor beyond God's control. Perhaps God didn't even want to answer our prayer, because He knew we were asking for something that would harm us in the end, but He just had no power to stop it!

We can be grateful that God is omnipotent. Nothing is outside His control. He is Lord of everything. He is more powerful than anything. There is nothing He cannot do.

> Ah Lord GOD! Behold, You have made the
> heavens and the earth by Your great power and
> by Your outstretched arm! Nothing is too
> difficult for You (Jer. 32:17).

Self-sufficient

If God is Lord of everything, nothing remains that is not His. That is to say, God lacks nothing. He is not in need of anything. If everything is His, there is nothing we could give Him that He does not already own. This is confusing for many people today. Some see God as a selfish and needy person who begs people to love Him. Other people might think that we have to do good works in order to pacify the anger of God. Others think we have to do things for God in order to get things from Him. Known as the "prosperity gospel," this is one of the most damaging heresies that currently faces the Christian church. A prosperity gospel preacher might say something like, "God wants to work in your life, but He can't unless you sow your seed of faith" (by which they mean you must donate to their organization). This is completely false. God does not accept bribes. He lacks nothing, and there is nothing we can do or give in order to commit God to giving us what we want.

> For every beast of the forest is Mine, the cattle

on a thousand hills. I know every bird of the mountains, and everything that moves in the field is Mine. If I were hungry I would not tell you, for the world is Mine, and all it contains (Ps. 50:10-12).

If God is Lord of everything, and He lacks nothing, then why did He create anything in the first place? Because it pleased Him to do so. He is a good Lord who takes pleasure in the things over which He is Lord. When God created everything, He called it good (Gen. 1:31). All things were created by Him and for Him (Col. 1:16). He exults over His people and rejoices over them with sounds of joy (Zeph. 3:17).

Father

In the Bible God is often referred to as our Father. He also calls Himself our Father (Mal. 1:6, 2:10), and Paul said that we are God's children (Acts 17:28). The fact that God calls Himself our Father emphasizes a relational aspect of God. Even though He is Creator and Lord, He is also Father. It means that God didn't just create everything to sit back and watch it from distance. He doesn't just want to rule over it like a power-hungry tyrant. He wants to care for us like a good father cares for his children.

Not everyone has had a good experience or relationship with their biological father. Because of this, some people don't relate well with the idea of God being our Heavenly Father. They might even have negative thoughts associated with that concept. We must understand, however, that when God calls Himself our Father, He means it in terms of a good and intimate relationship. As a good Father, He desires for us to know Him personally and intimately. He loves us and cares for us.

> Grace to you and peace from God our Father (1 Cor. 1:3).

> See how great a love the Father has bestowed on us, that we would be called children of God (1 John 3:1).

> I have loved you with an everlasting love; Therefore I have drawn you with lovingkindness (Jer. 31:3).

Our Need

One of the first turning points that must be made, when hearing the gospel, is acknowledging our need for God. We don't just need to know whether He exists. We don't just need to know things about Him. We need Him. We are completely and utterly dependent on God for everything. Paul said, "In Him we live and move and exist" (Acts 17:28). We need Him like we need light to see. Without him we grope aimlessly through darkness. This is why Paul refers to those that don't know God as being blind, and why coming to God is like turning from darkness to light (Acts 26:18). "God is Light," after all; and there is no darkness in Him (1 John 1:5).

Only when we realize our utter dependence on God and desperate need for Him will it matter that we've been separated from Him, which we will read about in the next chapter. Only when we realize that He is the only light will we realize how deep the darkness is without Him. Only when we truly sense our need for Him will it matter that He's made the way for us to be restored to Him. Do you sense your need for God? Does your soul thirst for Him? If so, read on. You will find your deepest desires fulfilled in knowing Him. He is not far from you (Acts 17:26), and He urges everyone to seek Him while He can be found (Isa. 55:6).

Summary

The good news begins with God because all things begin with God. The good news also ends with God, because He is the end of all things (Isa. 44:6). It will take an eternity to learn everything about a God who has already existed for an eternity.

In this chapter we focused on the things that the apostles said about God in the gospel sermons in the book of Acts, but this is only the beginning of the journey. The journey begins now, and it will never end. Will you join the millions of believers that have gone before you, who have made it their life's main ambition to know the God Who is Creator, Lord, and Father? Do you thirst for the living God? Do you desire to know Him?

Reflection Questions

Many different concepts were used above to describe God. Which ones were the most memorable for you?

Are there aspects about God, as described above, that are confusing to you?

If you could ask God anything, what would you ask Him?

Do you sense a desire within yourself to know God and be known by Him?

CHAPTER THREE

MAN

Introduction

What is man? Where did we come from? How did we get here? Why are we here? Do we have a purpose? These questions are as old as humanity itself. Many people have spent their entire lives seeking to understand the fundamental essence of our nature and the reasons for our existence.

In this chapter, we will look at what the Bible says about mankind. Specifically, we will look at how we got here, why we are here, what went wrong, and whether or not there is any hope left for us. At times this chapter will seem quite dark; but do not despair. There is light at the end of the tunnel. Read to the end in order to find it.

Created

When describing God, we began with Him being the Creator because that is the first thing He reveals to us about Himself. In the same way, the first thing He reveals about us is that we are created. In Genesis 1:26, God said, "Let us make man in Our image." Paul referred to this when he said that God created "from one man every nation of mankind to live on all the face of the earth" (Acts 17:26).

What does it mean to be created in God's image? The book of Genesis was originally written in the Hebrew language, and the Hebrew word translated as "image" refers to a shadow or resemblance (Strong 1890b, 99, "6754"). A shadow's shape, size, and movement bring attention to the object it resembles and tells us certain things about it. Similarly, being made in the image of God means there are things about us that reflect our Creator and make it possible for us to have a relationship with Him.

Children of God

Another way to think about being created in the image of God is to consider how children are in the image of their biological parents. There are similarities, both physically and in terms of personality, that point back to the parents. This does not mean that children are the same as their parents, nor that they are born with all of the same knowledge and experience as their parents. The similarities make it possible for children and parents to share an intimate relationship with one another. It is the natural tendency among children to look to their parents for specific emotional and physical needs, and it is the natural tendency among parents to meet these needs for their children. It should be no surprise, then, that Paul, when considering how we are created by God, concludes that we are all the "children of God," and that God is our Father (Acts 17:29).

This is a really good place to start, when thinking about mankind and how we relate to God. There are many people who believe that God does not exist. There are others who believe there is no way to be certain that God exists. When we think about humanity as being created in the image of God, it means there is something in the essence of our very nature that draws us to our Creator. There are certain needs we have that can only be met by our spiritual Father. These needs might be suppressed and unrealized by us, in the same way that the natural relationship between parents and children can be broken (by negligent parents, rebellious children, or both). But the need is still there. Being created by God, in His image, means our existence points back to God and we have a built-in need for a relationship with Him. There are real psychological problems that result from abuse or neglect among children. In the same way, there are very serious spiritual consequences that come from a severed relationship with God.

Paul said we were created so that we would seek God (Acts 17:27). It's the ultimate purpose of our existence. This is why Jesus said that eternal life is knowing God (John 17:3). Some people, when they hear terms like "eternal life," think about what happens after death. According to Jesus, eternal life begins the moment we are restored to God. The moment we enter into an intimate relationship with God, where we know Him and are known by Him (Gal. 4:9). It's not about a life that begins after we die. It's about life that begins right now and lasts forever. It's life in its purest sense; the way it was meant to be.

Sin

In the book of Acts, sin is often mentioned without definition because the audience is Jewish.

The Jews had grown up hearing about sin and knew what their Scriptures said about it. It did not need to be explained to them. What about those that don't have that understanding? Can someone who doesn't know God sin against Him? Yes. Can someone sin if he doesn't even know what sin is? Again, yes.

When Paul preached to a non-Jewish audience in Athens, he addressed this. The people in Athens worshiped all sorts of idols, and they were likely very unfamiliar with many of the terms used by the Jews. They didn't have the same background, upbringing, or beliefs. Still, even though they were ignorant of the Scriptures, Paul told them that God called them to repent because judgment was coming (Acts 17:30-31).

In the same way, you may or may not have a previous understanding of what sin is. You might have never heard the word. Even if you have, you may have a misunderstanding about what it is. Either way, God will hold you accountable. So it's really important to understand what sin is.

The New Testament Scriptures were originally written in Greek, and the Greek word for "sin" means to err, or to "miss the mark" (Strong 1890a, 10, "264"). As far as missing the mark, think of it like you're trying to throw a spear, or shoot an arrow, and it misses the target. The word gives the sense that with God there is a right path and a wrong path. There is the center of a target, and there is the outside of the target. When we disobey Him and rebel against Him, we have erred. We have gone down the wrong path. We have missed the mark of God's perfection. We have sinned.

In Genesis 3, Eve was tempted to eat of a tree that God had forbidden her and her husband, Adam, to eat from. Eve gave in to this temptation and ate from the tree. She then gave some to Adam, who also ate from it. Both of them were immediately ashamed. This is the first sin that ever happened (Gen. 3:1-8). They erred. Took the wrong path. They missed the mark. They fell.

The story in Genesis 3 is the story of how sin came into the world, but it's not the story of the only sin that ever happened. The Bible says that sin didn't stop there. Instead, because of that first sin, sin entered into the world and spread to all of us. Everyone is under this curse of sin. No one is righteous. No one seeks God on their own. All have turned aside and gone their own way (Rom. 3:9-12, 5:12).

This problem of sin isn't just a problem for Adam and Eve. It's not a problem for those other people. It's a problem for all of us. The Bible says that all of us have sinned. Have you ever lied, cheated, stolen, lusted, been jealous of someone else's possessions, or dishonored your parents? The Bible calls these things sins, and all of us have been guilty of most—if not all—of them. Even if we had only committed one of them, the Bible says that we would be guilty of the all of them (James 2:10). Sin is sin, and the consequences of sin are very serious.

As we read about these consequences below, it will be important to remember a couple of things. First, remember that you were created to have an intimate relationship with the God who created you. He is your heavenly Father, who made you in His image so that this relationship would be possible. Second, remember that we have all sinned. We have all turned against God, gone down the wrong path, and missed the mark. We've been separated from God. This applies to you, as well as to everyone else who has ever lived. No one is exempt. Third, remember that this is not the end of the story. Hope is coming, but we won't comprehend the value of that hope until we've comprehended the consequences of our sin.

Godless

When Adam and Eve sinned, an exchange

was made. They exchanged their relationship with God for a fleeting desire. They could no longer be in God's presence (Gen. 3:22-24). The relationship was severed. They became separated from God. In other words, they became godless (Acts 2:23). In the same way, all of us, because of sin, were separated from God. We turned away from Him in pursuit of our own desires, exchanging all of His eternal benefits with temporary things.

Idolatrous

When we desire anything more than the one true God, that other thing has become a god to us. This is idolatry (Acts 17:16, 23; 1 John 2:15-17;). To be godless, in one sense, means to live apart from God. But in another sense, it really means we've created other gods that we pursue instead of God. This is why those who don't know God can be called godless and idolatrous at the same time.

Idolatry goes against everything we were created for. We were not created to have an intimate relationship with pleasure, riches, power, overindulgence, or the approval of men. These things may provide some temporary sense of fulfillment or gratification, but they can't fill our deepest longings for God. These little gods are no gods at all. There is only one God, and as long as we reject Him, we sin against Him. As long as we reject Him, we cannot live life the way it was intended to be lived. We will forever have a second-rate existence, a life full of sinful pleasures but absent of the deeper meaning our soul craves.

Enslaved

One of the lies of idolatry is the belief that our deepest desires can be satisfied by anything other than God. In reality, an idol is a counterfeit god that makes promises it can't keep. The rewards are minimal, temporary, and always leave us wanting more. Just like an addiction, we will get just enough pleasure to keep us hooked, but never enough to satisfy us completely. We're left with an empty promise. It'll tell us that we could be more satisfied if we had a little more. Just a little more. No matter what it costs. No matter how much time, money, relationships, or physical health we have to sacrifice for it. Just get a little more. Maybe then the rewards will be greater. Maybe then we will be satisfied and complete. We're left waiting for a payoff that'll never come.

When the inadequate pleasures of one pursuit dry up and leave us unsatisfied, we'll deceive ourselves into thinking that we are still free. After all, can't we just switch to something else more satisfying? Maybe we've become unsatisfied climbing the corporate ladder in pursuit of success and power. Maybe we've become unsatisfied trying to be the perfect wife to a husband that will never see us the way we want him to. So how about something else? Have we considered our health lately? Have we considered this new diet, or that new work-out routine? What about shopping? Aren't there more things we can buy to make ourselves happy? What about sports? Couldn't we be happier if we spent more time following every player, team, and match for every sport that we enjoy? How about some other hobby that we can spend all our time obsessing about? And on and on we go, attempting to fill the void we have with other things, relentlessly and desperately attempting to block out the deeper truth we feel—that we were made for something more than this.

By the time we realize the trick, we might feel as if we've given up everything and we've got nothing left. The things we thought would help us be free have enslaved us. These false gods have over-promised and under-delivered, and in the meantime they've taken all we have. We never got the ultimate satisfaction we sought. We never felt as free as we expected we would. Things didn't turn out the way we planned.

This is why Paul talks about returning to God in terms of being "freed from all things" (Acts 13:39). Knowing God isn't just an option to consider. It's what we were made for. We can't survive without Him. We need God more than anything. When we don't have Him, we end up trying to fill that absence with other things. We turn other interests into cute little gods, and then try to get from them what only God can give us. These false gods cannot give us what we seek, no matter how much we give them. As long as we continue on this path, we will be forever enslaved.

Wicked

The Bible calls people that don't believe in God wicked (Acts 3:26, 17:5, 24:15). You might think this word just means "bad," "evil," "immoral," or "sinful." It does mean those things, but there's more to it than that. In Acts 3:26, when Peter talks about "wicked ways," the root word implies "great trouble," "intense desire," or "pain" (Thayer, Grimm, and Wilke 1889, 531). This same word can mean all of those things, which seems appropriate.

Imagine a hypothetical scenario where you believe that salt water is the only option for quenching thirst. You have a real need for hydration, but instead of getting what your body really needs, you fill your body with salt water. The problem is that there is too much salt, and not enough water, in the mixture. You'll be putting way more salt into your body than the water can expel. As a result, you become more and more thirsty, with an increasingly intense desire. And since you hypothetically believe that salt water is the cure for thirst, you're increasingly *intense desire* is directed at the wrong thing. You're in *great trouble,* because this will lead to *painful* physical problems and eventually death.

In the same way, since we were created for the purpose of being in a relationship with God, it's our most basic and essential need. Wickedness is when we've tricked ourselves into believing that something else can satisfy that need and we pursue that thing with intense desire as if it were God. Like salt water, it will only lead to more harm. Since we've convinced ourselves that some other thing can satisfy this desire in us, the realization of continued dissatisfaction will lead to increasingly intense, but misdirected, desires—which leads into the next section.

Perverse

When we have convinced ourselves that we

can find satisfaction for our deepest desires in something besides God, we will become increasingly dependent on that something. This unhealthy dependency on increasingly intense, but misdirected, desires can cause these desires to take on new forms. This is why it has been said that addiction is progressive. The hit is never as good the second time. You need a bit more. And then a bit more. Until you wake up one day in places you never expected to, associating with people you never wanted to, doing things you never thought you'd do.

The first chapter in the book of Romans maps out this progression. Because the world rejected God, they became "vain in their imaginations, and their foolish heart was darkened." They found other things to worship. This resulted in uncleanness, lust, envy, murder, and other "vile affections" that were against nature. As these desires increase, and as they continue to degrade, it can lead us to perverse thoughts, desires, and / or behaviors— things that we never expected, that go against our own conscience, and that we are ashamed of (Rom. 1:21, 23-24, 26, 29).

In the Bible, one of the more astounding examples of this is when the Jews got Pilate to put Jesus to death. According to the Scriptures, it is a sin to murder (Exod. 20;13). They had found no fault with Him. They could bring no accusations against Him. But they hated him. They wanted Him dead. Their hatred for Jesus was so strong that it led them to do whatever it would take to put an end to Him, no matter how perverse, including sinning against God by committing murder (Acts 3:15-16, 10:39).

In Darkness

God is light (1 John 1:5). To walk with Him is to walk in light. Turning to God is described in the Bible as turning "from darkness to light" (Acts 26:19). To reject Him is to be in darkness. Eternal damnation is referred to as outer darkness (Matt. 22:13). Just as eternal life starts now for those that know God, eternal damnation has already begun for everyone who walks in darkness. Just as we cannot see without light, so we cannot truly live without God. It's as if we are walking around in utter darkness, groping with outstretched hands because we are unable to see anything. This is why Jesus calls men blind that do not really know God (Matt. 23:19; John 12:37-40).

Separation from God is as real as darkness and as bitter as chasing after things that cannot satisfy.

The next three sections will focus on three aspects of our spiritual condition that have profound significance to the gospel story. Keep these in mind as you read through the rest of this book.

Legally Guilty

The Bible says that sin is the same as lawlessness in God's eyes (1 John 3:4). When we sin against God, we break His law. Even if a person only ever sins once, they are guilty of breaking the whole law (James 2:10). When we break His law, we incur debt upon ourselves. The Bible speaks about a "record of debt" that stands against us (Col. 2:14). God has kept track of our sins, and the debt for those sins must be re-payed. We are legally guilty.

Spiritually Dead

Knowing God is the only thing that can make us truly alive (John 17:3). Separation from God is separation from life. God told Adam that he would die if he disobeyed Him (Gen. 3:3). This is the same consequence that all of us face because of our sin. The Bible says that death first came into the world through sin, and that the wages of sin is death (Rom. 5:12, 6:23). By our very nature we are children of wrath who are dead in our sins (Eph. 2:1-3). We are spiritually dead.

Awaiting Judgment

The Bible makes it very clear that judgment is coming for those that have rejected God and sinned against Him. This judgment is described in many ways, including death (Rom. 6:23), blindness (Acts 26:18), darkness (Matt. 22:13; Acts 26:18), utter destruction (Acts 3:23), everlasting destruction (2 Thess. 1:9), eternal punishment (Matt. 25:46), lake of fire and eternal torment (Rev. 20:10, 21:15), and weeping and gnashing of teeth (Matt. 13:50).

Legally Guilty
Spiritually Dead
Awaiting Judgment

Can anything be done to avoid this? Can we just change our life and do better? Do more good to pay God back for all the bad we've done? Unfortunately, the Bible says that our good behavior will never add up enough to restore all that has been lost (Ps. 51:5; Isa. 64:6). Even if we stopped doing any kind of wrong, from this moment on, it wouldn't erase the wrong we've already done. And even if there were a way to erase our past wrongs on our own, it wouldn't change the fact that we are already spiritually dead. Simply paying back the debt doesn't give us new life. What, then, can be done? Is there any hope?

Hope is Coming

Even though there is nothing we can do to save ourselves, God has provided a solution. This is the hope of the gospel. The gospel message isn't a call to live a better life. It isn't a call to try and pay God back for all the bad we've done. It isn't a call to legalism. It is a message of hope. All of the debts accumulated by your sin against God can be wiped away completely, forgotten, as if they were never there. We can have life instead of death. This is why the apostles, when sharing the gospel, called out so often to repent, turn back to Him, receive forgiveness, and be saved from judgment (Acts 2:38-40, 4:12, 5:31, 10:43, 13:38, 26:18).

Summary

This chapter describes the devastating condition of mankind. We were created by God to know Him intimately as our heavenly Father. Sin separated us from God, leading to all sorts of eternally dire consequences. Judgment is coming for all those who have broken God's law, and all of us are guilty. We are legally guilty, spiritually dead, and awaiting judgment, and there's nothing that we can do about it on our own.

Yet there is hope. The apostles call out over and over again that we can find forgiveness, life, and escape God's judgment. But how?

Reflection Questions

One of the ways God refers to Himself is as our Father, and us as His children. Do you have a hard time thinking that God could love you or want to have a relationship with you?

Many terms were used to describe the condition of man because of sin. Which ones were the most memorable to you?

What are your thoughts about your own spiritual condition?

As you read about how the Bible describes the nature of man and reflected on your own life, what aspects of this chapter resonated with you those most?

CHAPTER FOUR

JESUS

Introduction

Despite the tragic reality that we have separated ourselves from God, and despite the fact that there is nothing we can do to restore ourselves to Him, there is hope. This hope has a name: Jesus Christ. Jesus is "the hope of the promise made by God" (Acts 26:6). In this chapter we will look at the person of Jesus, and we will begin to pave the way to a better understanding of how He is the only hope we have to be restored to God. Hope is coming, and hope is here. Jesus gives us that hope. Who is Jesus?

Sent

The first thing that was revealed about God was that He was the Creator of all things. The first thing that was revealed about man was that man was created by God. What about Jesus? How shall we begin to describe Him? This is how John starts off his gospel:

> In the beginning was the Word, and the Word was with God, and the Word was God. He was in the beginning with God. All things came into being through Him, and apart from Him nothing came into being that has come into being. In Him was life, and the life was the Light of men...And the Word became flesh, and dwelt among us, and we saw His glory, glory as of the only begotten from the Father, full of grace and truth (John 1:1-4, 14).

Jesus was not created. He was sent. He has always existed. He is eternal. He created all things. He is "Lord of all" (Acts 10:36). He is God[1]. In order to enter this world in human form, He "took on flesh," being born of the virgin Mary. He did not begin to exist when He came into this world. He existed long before then.

Jesus was sent to bless us, grant us repentance

---

1   For more information on the nature of God, please see Appendix 1.

and forgiveness of sins, and help us turn from our wicked ways (Acts 3:26, 5:31). His coming should not have been a surprise. The Jewish Scriptures clearly foretold His coming, and the first disciples followed Jesus because they understood Him to be the fulfillment of these prophecies.

Anointed One

"Messiah," "Christ," and "Anointed One" are words used in the Bible that have the same meaning. "Messiah" comes from Hebrew and "Christ" comes from Greek. Both words mean "Anointed One."

The Hebrew Scriptures of the Old Testament are filled with prophecies of a coming Messiah, an Anointed One. He would be a descendant of King David (2 Sam. 7:12-16), would be born in Bethlehem (Mic. 5:2), and would be born of a virgin (Isa. 7:14). He would be a prophet (Deut. 18:15-19), a Nazarene (Isa. 11:1), a healer (Isa. 35:5-6), and a light for the nations of the world (Isa. 42:1-6). He would suffer (Ps. 69), and would be a willing sacrifice (Gen. 22:1-18). These are just some examples of the many prophecies about the coming Anointed One.

When Jesus began preaching and performing miracles, it became clear to many that He was the fulfillment of these prophecies. They forsook all and followed after Him. When the apostles preached about Jesus, this was one of the things they emphasized the most—that He was indeed the Christ, the Anointed One, the Messiah of the prophecies who would set the people free (Acts 2:36, 3:6, 3:18, 3:20, 10:36, 26:23).

Savior

We were unable to save ourselves from the condemnation of a just God. Our sins were stacked against us like debts that we could not pay. We needed salvation. We needed a Savior. This is why Jesus came. Because of what He did (which we will read about in the following chapters), salvation is now freely available. Jesus is not just *a* savior. He is *the* Savior. He's not just an option to consider. There are no other options. He is the only One that can save us.

> "There is no other name under heaven that has been given among men by which we must be saved" (Acts 4:12).

> He is the one whom God exalted to His right hand as a Prince and a Savior, to grant repentance to Israel, and forgiveness of sins (Acts 5:31).

Of Him all the prophets bear witness that
through His name everyone who believes in
Him receives forgiveness of sins (Acts 10:43).

Servant

Imagine someone being sent by a king to a
foreign country to be his representative. Would he
not be sent off well? Would he not be introduced in
some grandiose manner that would demonstrate the
power and might of his king's kingdom? Would he
not be adorned in fine clothing and jewelry? Would
he not have musicians and dancers to go before him
to announce his coming? Would he not carry about
him a sense of self-importance, serving at the mercy
of the king and being entrusted by the king with
such a significant position? Would he not stay in
the finest establishments, dine in the most excellent
restaurants, with the most important people, and
have body guards to establish a barrier between
himself and the common folk?

Jesus did none of these things. Jesus was not
born to a rich family. He was not born to a rich
community. He was born of the virgin Mary, who
was engaged to a man named Joseph. They were
from Nazareth, a small town that was not well
respected. When a man named Nathanael first
heard of Jesus, and that He came from Nazareth, he

was surprised. He said, "Can any good thing come out of Nazareth?" (John 1:46). Jesus, being God, could have chosen any scenario for entering into this world, yet He chose this humble path of a servant. The apostles often brought attention to this fact when they preached the gospel (Acts 2:22, 3:6, 4:10).

Jesus did not come as a proud ruler demanding servants who would obey and not ask questions. He did not come with a mighty fist to crush those who opposed Him. Instead, He came as a servant. The Bible says that even though Jesus was in the form of God before He came to earth, He emptied Himself, humbled Himself and took on the form of a servant (Phil. 2:6-8). Jesus Christ—God, the Messiah and Lord of all—came as a servant.

Perfect

Jesus lived a perfect life. He was blameless and without sin. He was holy and righteous (Acts 3:14). Just because He was God in the flesh doesn't mean that He didn't experience temptation like the rest of us. In fact, the Bible says that He was tempted in all the ways that we are tempted. He was tempted by Satan with "every temptation" over the course of forty days (Luke 4:2, 13). Stumbling blocks were put in the way of His mission (Matt.

16:23). He struggled when faced with hardship (Luke 22:42). In all of these things, He persevered and remained sinless. Not only was His righteousness necessary for His mission, but it's also wonderful for us to know that Jesus understands our struggles and sympathizes with us in them.

> For we do not have a high priest who cannot sympathize with our weaknesses, but One who has been tempted in all things as [we are, yet] without sin (Heb. 4:15)

What He Said and Did

Jesus preached about His kingdom. He taught about the condition of man, the problem of sin, and the need for repentance. He opposed the hypocritical religious rulers of the day who honored God with their lips while their hearts were far from Him (Matt. 15:7). He taught His disciples to pursue lives of love, humility, sacrifice, and purpose. He taught them how to pray. He explained Who He was and why He came. He foretold of His own death, and foretold of the coming persecution for those that would follow Him. He promised His followers life, joy, peace, reconciliation with God, and a place with Him in the coming Kingdom at the end of the age.

Jesus cared for the poor. He healed the sick. He gave sight to the blind. He gave the lame strength to walk again. He touched those who were outcast. He had compassion on the weak. He wept with those who were sorrowful. He ate and drank with sinners. He lived a perfect and sinless life. He performed many miracles as proof of Who He was. He was both God and man, divinity and humanity. "In Him was life, and the life was the Light of men" (John 1:4).

> "Jesus the Nazarene, a man attested to you by God with miracles and wonders and signs which God performed through Him in your midst, just as you yourselves know" (Acts 2:22).

> "You know of Jesus of Nazareth, how God anointed Him with the Holy Spirit and with power, and how He went about doing good and healing all who were oppressed by the devil, for God was with Him" (Acts 10:38).

Summary

Jesus was not created; He was sent. He went around preaching the gospel, doing miracles, and calling everyone to repent and believe. He is the Christ, the Anointed One, holy and righteous.

Jesus is perfect and we are not. We are legally guilty, spiritually dead, and awaiting judgment. These are serious problems. In the following chapters, we will be look at how Jesus' crucifixion, resurrection, and ascension provide the only solution. These essential truths of the gospel will shed light on how we can be set free from sin and death forever.

Reflection Questions

After reading this chapter, how would you describe Who Jesus Is?

Where did Jesus come from?

Were there things in this chapter that you did not know before about Jesus?

If you could ask Jesus anything, what would you ask Him?

CHAPTER FIVE

CRUCIFIXION

Introduction

Jesus preached truth about God, His kingdom, the fallen state of man, and the need for repentance and forgiveness. He preached against hypocrisy and promoted love and compassion for the weak. He performed many miracles. He traveled from village to village, blessing all those that would receive Him and bringing joy to many. But that was not the main reason He came. The main reason He came was to provide us with a way to be restored to God.

Rejected

Jesus' message and activities weren't welcomed by everyone. The religious leaders of the day were proud men who were great in their own eyes. They considered themselves to be an elite class worthy of esteem by all men. When the Messiah came, they fully expected to be approved and honored by Him. They expected Him to be on their team. Instead, Jesus opposed their hypocrisy publicly. He called out their misuses of Scripture and their exploitation of the poor and weak. He called them "whitewashed tombs" (Matt. 23:27). He completely undermined their authority in front of the people and jeopardized their previously unquestioned rank among them.

Jesus did not live the way the religious leaders expected the Anointed One to live. He ate and drank in the homes of sinners. He showed mercy on those that they considered unworthy. He performed miracles on the Sabbath Day. He had no intention of creating a military uprising to free Israel from Roman rule. None of these things fit into their idea about what the Messiah should be like. Yet people loved Him, and many were following Him. In their view, He had to be stopped.

It is a terrible thing when pride makes one

blind to the reality that stares them in the face. The things Jesus did and taught proved that He was the Messiah. His miracles were irrefutable. His teaching was superior than anything they had ever heard before (John 7:46). It should have given the religious leaders pause to think that a man such as this would be opposed to them. It should have caused them to reevaluate their standing before God. As their sin was revealed, it should have caused them to repent, but they were unwilling. Even though "He had performed so many signs before them, [yet] they were not believing in Him" (John 12:37). Instead, they sought to put an end to Him.

At first, they tried to debate with Him. They tried to challenge His understanding of the Scriptures. They tried to make Him pick sides in their own disputes. They tried to poke holes in His teaching, to find a way to win the people back. Yet He demonstrated superior teaching at every turn. Eventually, they stopped trying. They realized they could not win this way. "No one was able to answer Him a word, nor did anyone dare from that day on to ask Him another question" (Matt. 22:46).

When disputing with Him publicly didn't work, they decided the only way to fix this problem was to kill Him.

Foretold

When the apostles spoke about the rejection and crucifixion of the Messiah, they emphasized the fact that these were not unforeseen events. They were always part of God's plan. For example:

> "This Man, delivered over *by the predetermined plan and foreknowledge of God,* you nailed to a cross by the hands of godless men and put Him to death…the things which *God announced beforehand by the mouth of all the prophets,* that His Christ would suffer, He has thus fulfilled" (Acts 2:23; 3:18; emphasis added).

Jesus always knew that His public ministry was leading up to this. He spoke often about it (Mark 8:31). He wasn't caught off-guard by His being rejected, betrayed, arrested, tortured, and killed. The Scriptures had prophecied that it would happen.

Jesus said that no one took His life from Him, but that He willingly gave it up (John 10:18). The news about Christ's crucifixion should not cause us to feel sorry for Jesus as some kind of helpless victim. Rather, it should cause us to be amazed and confounded by the immeasurable love of God that He would send His own Son to die on our behalf. It should cause us to think on the love of Jesus, that

He would endure such suffering for us.

> By this the love of God was manifested in us,
> that God has sent His only begotten Son into the
> world so that we might live through Him (1
> John 4:9)

> Fixing our eyes on Jesus, the author and
> perfecter of faith, who for the joy set before
> Him endured the cross, despising the shame, and
> has sat down at the right hand of the throne of
> God (Heb. 12:2)

Betrayed

Judas was one of Jesus' disciples who was different than the others. In his interactions with Jesus recorded in the Bible, it is never recorded that He professed love for Jesus, faith in Him, or loyalty to Him like many of the others had done. The Bible also calls him a thief, stating that he was the one who carried their money box and that he used to steal from it (John 12:6).

This Judas made a secret plan with the chief priests. He knew they wanted to kill Jesus, and he went to them privately, asking them what they would give him to betray Jesus to them. They offered him thirty pieces of silver, and he accepted.

This, too, was no surprise. Scripture had prophecied of a betrayal of the Messiah (Zech.

11:12-13), and Jesus had told His disciples very early on in His ministry that one of them would betray Him (John 6:70-71). On the night of His betrayal and arrest, as He ministered to His disciples by washing their feet and sharing one last meal with them, He reminded them of what was about to happen. He named Judas as His betrayer, then sent him away, saying, "What you do, do quickly" (John 13:27). He then began to share with the other disciples how they would all "fall away" that night and be scattered when He was taken.

Arrested

On the night that Jesus was betrayed, Judas led "a large crowd with swords and clubs" (Matt. 26:47) to arrest Him. Jesus instructed His disciples to not fight back. As they took Jesus away, the disciples fled. Next, Jesus would face six trials.

First, He was taken to the home of Annas, who had formerly been a high priest and who still apparently held a high position of influence. He was questioned about His teaching, and when He answered back, one of the men struck Him on the face (John 18:12-14, 19-22).

Second, He was bound and led to Caiaphas, the high priest. Scribes and elders had gathered, and it was their goal to find some way to accuse

Him. Many came forward, but their testimonies could not be corroborated. Then Caiaphas commanded Jesus to state plainly whether He was the Christ, and He confirmed it. This was apparently sufficient reason to have him killed, for Caiaphas tore his own robes, called Jesus a blasphemer, and the people present agreed that He deserved death. They "spat in His face and beat Him with their fists; and others slapped Him" (Matt. 26:65-67).

Third, the next morning, they reconvened and reiterated their agreement that Jesus must die. They "bound Him, and led Him away and delivered Him to Pilate the governor" (Matt. 27:2). The Jews at this time were under Roman rule, and they were unable to pronounce a death sentence on their own. They needed the sentence to come from a Roman court.

Fourth, He was brought before Pilate, the governor of Judea. Many of the chief priests and elders had come and were accusing Him of many things, but Jesus did not answer any of them. When Pilate asked Jesus directly whether He was the King of the Jews, He answered that He was. Pilate was amazed that Jesus wasn't trying to defend Himself or escape imprisonment or death (Matt. 27:11-15). Pilate didn't think Jesus had done anything worthy of death, but the people were insistent. When Pilate heard that Jesus was from Galilee, he thought he had found his way out of this mess, which leads to the next trial.

Fifth, Pilate sent Jesus to Herod, the ruler of Galilee. Herod had heard of Jesus and hoped to see a miracle or two. He questioned Jesus for some time, and the chief priests and elders were continuing to accuse Him. Jesus did not respond or do any miracles, and Herod apparently became unsatisfied. Still, he was unwilling to pronounce the sentence of death on Him, so he sent Jesus back to Pilate (Luke 23:8-12).

Sixth, Jesus was brought again before Pilate. Pilate tried to reason with the people, but they would not listen. Then he apparently tried to satisfy them mocking Jesus publicly. The Romans soldiers stripped Him. They spit on Him and beat Him. They blind-folded Him and slapped Him in the face. They made Him wear a scarlet robe, a crown of thorns, and a reed, and then they bowed before Him in mock-allegiance. Pilate brought Him out before the people like this, and mocked Him, saying, "Behold the man!" (John 19:5). This was not enough for the people. It got to the point where the people were just shouting, "Crucify Him!" over and over again (Luke 23:21). Eventually Pilate gave in and gave the people what they wanted.

Crucified

Crucifixion is a horrendous, painful, and shameful method of public capital punishment. The person being crucified, having previously been stripped and beaten, is nailed to a wooden cross and left to die on public display. It is torture, slow and agonizing. Those hanging on the cross must lift themselves up in order to breathe. This is extremely painful because the entire weight of their body is being held up by their hands and feet, which are attached to the wood by nails. It is also very exhausting, and can last for days. Eventually, the person is simply no longer able to lift themselves, and so it is death by asphyxiation.

When someone was being crucified by Rome, they were forced to carry their cross to the place of execution after they had been stripped and beaten. Jesus' beatings were apparently much more severe than usual, because they had to ask a man named Simon to help carry His cross (Matt. 27:31-32).

He was taken to a place called Golgotha, and there they crucified the King of Kings and Lord of Lords, the Anointed One, Jesus the Christ. He was crucified along with two other criminals. They drove nails into His hands and His feet and left Him to die (John 19:17-18).

The Romans became impatient, and wanted Jesus and the two other criminals to die faster. They planned to come around and break their legs so that they could no longer lift themselves up to breathe. When they came to Jesus, however, He appeared to already be dead. To confirm whether He was dead, they pierced His side with a spear. Blood and water flowed out together (John 19:31-34).

A man named Joseph asked for the body of Jesus and saw to His burial. With the help of Nicodemus, Jesus was wrapped in linen cloth and buried in a tomb. A large stone was rolled over the entrance (John 19:38-42; Matt. 27:60).

Why?

Jesus knew this was going to happen. He told His disciples many times that it would happen, and that it was for this reason that He had come into the world. He went willingly. But why? Why did Jesus come to the earth to die? What does it mean?

Remember that everyone is a sinner. Sin is rejection of God and disobedience to His law. Sin results in complete and absolute separation from God. The punishment for sin is death (Rom. 3:23, 6:23). We were all **legally guilty** because of our sin, and we are unable to repay the debts stacked against.

Also remember that God is just. He exacts judgment on the guilty (Rom. 2:2). No one gets away with their sin. The price must be paid. No judge would be considered just if he were to sweep crimes under the rug. We would call that judge corrupt. God is not corrupt and cannot turn a blind eye to our sin.

Jesus came into this world to pay the price for our sins. He walked among us, was tempted just like we are tempted, and yet was completely without sin. He was perfect and holy, and yet He took our sins upon Himself and was punished in our place. It should have been us. We deserve the full punishment for our sins, but Jesus took our place.

His crucifixion was not an accident. It was part of the plan. It's why He came. His death on the cross was for us. The Bible says that God made Jesus "who knew no sin [to be] sin on our behalf" (2 Cor. 5:15), and that He became "a curse for us" (Gal. 3:13).

Isaiah 53 is perhaps one of the most well-known prophecies about the crucifixion of the Messiah and what it would mean for the world. Here are some portions of it:

He was despised and forsaken of men, A man of sorrows and acquainted with grief...Surely our griefs He Himself bore, And our sorrows He carried...He was pierced through for our transgressions, He was crushed for our iniquities; The chastening for our well-being [fell] upon Him, And by His scourging we are healed. All of us like sheep have gone astray, Each of us has turned to his own way; But the LORD has caused the iniquity of us all To fall on Him. He was oppressed and He was afflicted, Yet He did not open His mouth; Like a lamb that is led to slaughter, And like a sheep that is silent before its shearers, So He did not open His mouth. But the LORD was pleased To crush Him, putting [Him] to grief...As a result of the anguish of His soul, He will see [it and] be satisfied; By His knowledge the Righteous One, My Servant, will justify the many, As He will bear their iniquities (Isa. 53:3-7, 10-11).

The last thing that Jesus said on the cross was, "It is finished" (John 19:30). Jesus, being perfect and holy, bore our sins on the cross and paid for them. The legal guilt we carried because of our sins was resolved. The debt was repaid.

You Did It

One of the essential things that must happen, when hearing the gospel, is recognizing who is to blame for the torture and death of Jesus Christ. The

Jews aren't to blame. The Romans aren't the blame. Everyone is to blame. Sin isn't someone else's problem. Jesus' death was not for someone else. We did this. It was because of our sins, and because of God's unfathomable love and desire to be restored to His creation, that Jesus came to die for our sins.

The apostles were quick to pass the blame around to everyone who heard the gospel—even those who did not have any direct involvement in the actual arrest and crucifixion (Acts 2:36; 3:15). In other words, you did it. We all did. You disowned Him. We all did. You delivered Him over to be crucified and put the Prince of Life to death. We all did. We crucified the Messiah. It was because of our sin that He hung on the cross and died.

Summary

Jesus came to pay the price for our sins, and He was tortured, crushed, and killed for our sakes. Because of what He did, we can be restored back to God. The price has been paid for our many sins, so that we no longer have to remain legally guilty.

Does that mean that we are off the hook? That there are no more guilty, and that everyone goes to heaven? Not exactly. Something must happen in the present in order for us to receive the benefits of this transaction. That will be discussed in more detail in the "Conclusion" chapter.

The crucifixion of Jesus Christ is not the end of the gospel story. If it were, it would not be good news. In the following chapter, we will discuss why we would be completely without hope if this were the final chapter.

Reflection Questions

Why did Jesus die?

Was Jesus a victim? Was He surprised by the rejection of His people? Did He try to escape His death? If not, why not?

Who is to blame for Jesus' death?

What is the significance of Jesus' crucifixion, in terms of the gospel?

CHAPTER SIX

RESURRECTION

Introduction

The good news does not end with the death of Jesus Christ. If it did, it would not be very good news. If Jesus' death was the end of the story, then it would have devastatingly negative effects on the gospel. It wouldn't be called the gospel, because it wouldn't be good news. In fact, Paul wrote that if Jesus' death was the end of the story, our faith would be worthless, and followers of Jesus would be pitied more than anyone else who ever lived (1 Cor. 15:17,19). There would be no hope.

What is at Stake?

Let's think about what is at stake in this. What if Jesus didn't raise from the dead? What would that mean?

First, it would mean that Jesus wasn't Who He said He was. Jesus claimed to be the Messiah, and the Old Testament prophecied that the Messiah would not be able to stay in the grave. Isaiah 53:10 said that His days will be prolonged, and this is written after the account of His death in the same chapter. Psalm 16:10 prophecied that the Messiah would not be abandoned in death, and that His body will not "undergo decay." Peter referred to this passage when preaching about Jesus' resurrection (Acts 2:27). If Jesus didn't raise from the dead, He was not the Messiah, and He can't offer us any kind of salvation. Furthermore, if Jesus said He was the Messiah, and wasn't, that makes Him a liar. If Jesus was a liar, then He was a sinner. If He was a sinner, He would not have been worthy to offer Himself as a sacrifice for our sins.

Second, it would mean that our sins weren't fully paid for. Remember that the penalty for sin is physical and spiritual death. This eternal death sentence remains in force until it is carried out. The debt is owed until it is paid. It has power over those that are guilty of it as long as the guilt remains—power to cause death and keep us in the grave forever. Jesus bore our sins on the cross in order to free us from this debt completely. If it is true that the sins were fully paid for on the cross, then it wouldn't have been possible for Jesus to remain in the grave. What would be holding Him down, preventing His life, if the price for sin was completely paid? Sin would only have power to keep Him in the grave if the debt hadn't been fully paid. If Jesus had remained dead, it would mean that something is still owed. We would still be guilty.

Third, it would mean we have no hope of life. Jesus promised to give us life, and to personally raise us from the dead (John 6:40, 44, 54). If He had stayed dead, this would not be possible. A dead man cannot do anything. We would still be spiritually dead, because a dead man cannot make us spiritually alive. There would be no resurrection for us, because a dead man cannot raise us from the dead. Paul made it very clear how significantly and severely it would crush our faith if Jesus did not raise from the dead:

> If Christ has not been raised, then our preaching is vain, your faith also is vain. Moreover we are

even found [to be] false witnesses of God, because we testified against God that He raised Christ, whom He did not raise, if in fact the dead are not raised. For if the dead are not raised, not even Christ has been raised; and if Christ has not been raised, your faith is worthless; you are still in your sins. Then those also who have fallen asleep in Christ have perished. If we have hoped in Christ in this life only, we are of all men most to be pitied (1 Cor. 15:14-19).

This is very serious. He had to raise from the dead, or else all would be lost. When John described how the disciples didn't always understand Jesus' claim that He would rise from the dead, he wrote, "For as yet they did not understand the Scripture, that He must rise again" (John 20:9). Notice the word "must." He *must* rise again. This is a matter of necessity. If Jesus didn't raise from the dead, then Jesus would not be the Messiah. He would be a lying sinner. Our sins would not be paid for. We would have no hope.

Thanks be to God that this is not what happened. Jesus didn't stay dead, and that has made all the difference.

The Resurrection

Jesus rose three days after His death, just like

He said He would. He was seen by Mary Magdalene, along with other women who had come to bring spices to His grave. He walked with two other disciples while they walked on the road from Jerusalem to Emmaus, explaining to them all of the things in the Jewish Scriptures that spoke of Him. He appeared to the eleven disciples while they had locked themselves in an upper room. In order to convince them that it really was Him, and that He wasn't a ghost, He ate fish in front of them. Then He showed them the wounds in His hands and side. When Thomas felt these, He called Jesus his Lord and his God. The disciples worshiped Him. The full account of these things can be read in more detail in Matthew 28, Mark 16, Luke 24, and John 20.

This was not a quick appearance. His resurrection was not an apparition, or something that could be explained by temporary insanity or hallucinations. Jesus "presented Himself alive after His suffering, by many convincing proofs, appearing to them over a period of forty days and speaking of the things concerning the kingdom of God" (Acts 1:3). Paul wrote that Jesus appeared to more than five hundred people at the same time, after His resurrection (1 Cor. 15:6).

The evidence of Jesus' resurrection was

something that the apostles emphasized often when they shared this story with people. They never expected anyone to simply take their word for it. They weren't concerned that the listener would look into the facts and become convinced that it was some kind of manufactured conspiracy. They were confident, not only because they had seen Jesus risen, but the people listening had seen Him also. Peter often said "we are all witnesses" of the resurrection, including those to whom He was preaching (Acts 2:32, 3:15, 5:32). In Caesarea, Peter said "You yourselves know the things that took place" (Acts 10:37).

This is very bold. It's a challenge. It's an appeal to facts. Imagine Peter preaching to thousands of people, claiming that Jesus rose from the dead, and claiming that those people had seen it also. Well, if Jesus hadn't risen from the dead, this would be an easy message to refute, wouldn't it? Here is Peter saying, "You are all witnesses that Jesus rose from the dead. You all saw it. You know that this is true." He's confidently appealing to their knowledge of the facts. But what if it wasn't true? What if Jesus hadn't risen from the dead? What if Peter was making it up? Can you imagine anyone believing a message that appeals so strongly to facts, if the facts could be easily dismissed as false?

If these people hadn't really witnessed Jesus', then the message would have stopped dead in its tracks. If they hadn't seen Jesus risen, then Peter would have been lying, and they'd have known it. He would have said, "You saw Him raised," and they would have said, "No we didn't," and that would have been the end of it. It's a very bold way to preach, and it would be very simple to refute the message if it weren't true. But that isn't how people responded. No one denied His resurrection.

There were some that rejected the message, but never because they disagreed with the facts. Instead, they tried to pay off people to lie about it (Matt. 28:12). When that didn't work, they began imprisoning and beating Christians, and commanding them to not preach the message. When that didn't work, they set out to kill them (Acts 5:18, 28, 33). Why? Because they couldn't refute the fact that Jesus had risen.

The point here is simple. If the account of Jesus' resurrection could have been easily refuted, the Christian faith would not have survived until today. The message of the gospel would have been dead on arrival. Many continue to come to faith in Jesus Christ by researching the facts and becoming convinced that this really happened.

What does it mean?

It is truly amazing that Jesus rose from the dead. It's the most important miracle of all time. It's also much more than that. It's much more than a spectacle to be amazed by. It is a foundational part of the gospel story, and it has significant implications for us that cannot be overestimated.

First, the resurrection fulfills prophecy. The Scriptures prophecied that the Messiah would raise from the dead, and it came true. Jesus predicted that He would raise from the dead, which means He's not a liar. It proves that He really is the Messiah (Act 13:33; 17:31). It means that He spoke the truth, and we can trust what He said.

Second, it means that our sins really are fully paid for. As was written above – if Jesus had stayed dead, it would mean that sin still had power to keep Him in the grave. He could have only risen if sin had lost its power. This is why Peter said that Jesus put "an end to the agony of death, since it was impossible for Him to be held in its power" (Acts 2:24). What a tremendous thought! There is a present agony in being spiritually dead because of sin, and there is an eternal agony in being condemned to hell for it. Because Jesus completely paid off the debt, it was unable to hold Him in the grave. He rose because death no longer had power over Him, and He now provides a way of escape from this agony.

Third, it means that we have hope. Hope of new life, not only in this life, but in the life to come. Remember what the crucifixion accomplished. We were legally guilty, and Jesus paid that price for us, but that was only part of what was needed. We were still **spiritually dead**. Jesus rose so that we could receive the benefits of His resurrection, both in this life and in the life to come. Concerning the present, Jesus said, "I came that they might have life, and have it abundantly" (John 10:10). Paul wrote, "As Christ was raised from the dead through the glory of the Father, so we too might walk in newness of life" (Rom. 6:4). Concerning eternity, Jesus promised to raise His followers up on the last day (John 6:40), and Paul wrote that if Jesus hadn't risen from the dead, we would not have this hope (1 Cor. 15:16-19).

Summary

The crucifixion fully paid for our sins, so that we no longer have to bear the burden of that guilt before God. The resurrection demonstrates that Jesus is Who He said He was, that the sin was fully paid for, and that we can trust in Jesus' promise to give us life. The miracle of Jesus' resurrection is a factual event, and it is the validation of everything that He accomplished for us.

Reflection Questions

Did the disciples always know that Jesus would raise from the dead?

What if Jesus hadn't risen from the dead?

How many people saw Him after He had risen from the dead?

What is the significance of Jesus' resurrection, in terms of the gospel?

CHAPTER SEVEN

ASCENSION

Introduction

After the resurrection, Jesus spent forty more days with His disciples. At the end of those forty days, He gathered them together and spoke these final words:

> "All authority has been given to Me in heaven and on earth. Go therefore and make disciples of all the nations, baptizing them in the name of the Father and the Son and the Holy Spirit, teaching them to observe all that I commanded you; and lo, I am with you always, even to the end of the age" (Matt. 28:18-20).

While He was speaking these words, the

disciples watched as He was lifted off of the earth in a cloud until He was out of sight (Acts 1:9). After He was gone, the disciples worshiped Him, returned to the city, and began to proclaim everywhere and to everyone all of what they had seen and heard about Jesus (Luke 24:52, Mark 16:20).

Why didn't Jesus stay with us on earth forever? Why did He have to ascend back into heaven? What does it mean for His followers, that He is in heaven again? What is He doing now?

Why Did Jesus Have to Ascend?

Jesus told the disciples that He had to go away, and that it was to their advantage that He return to heaven so that He could send the Holy Spirit to them. The Holy Spirit would help them, comfort them, lead them into truth, and remind them of what He taught them (John 16:7-13). He would empower them to be bold witnesses of the gospel. He would do miracles through them. At Pentecost, the Holy Spirit came upon them like a rushing wind, and they began to proclaim the mighty works of God in various languages, which everyone listening understood in their own language. Thousands of people became followers of Jesus that day (Acts 1:4-8; 2:1-8, 41; 8:13; 19:11). From then until now, the Holy Spirit has continued to help Jesus' disciples know and experience God, understand the Scriptures, live bold lives of faith, and share the gospel with others.

Where is Jesus Now?

Jesus is in heaven sitting at the right hand of God. He has the absolute highest position of authority. He said that all authority on earth and in heaven was His. He is greater than any ruler or authority. His name is greater than any name. Everything is subject to Him, and every knee in heaven and earth will bow before Him (Acts 2:33, 3:21; Eph. 1:21-22; Phil. 2:9-10).

Jesus also said that He would always be with us (Matt. 28:20). He told us to abide in Him like a branch abides in a vine (John 15:1-4). Paul wrote that those who are joined to the Lord are one spirit with Him (1 Cor. 6:17). How can it be that Jesus is both in heaven and with us? How can we abide in Him, and be joined with Him, if He is in heaven?

One way to answer this is to point back to the fact that Jesus is God[2], and that God is not bound by space or time. He can be everywhere at once. However, another way to look at it is to consider this to be the work of the Holy Spirit, as mentioned

---

2   For more information on the nature of God, please see Appendix 1.

above. The Holy Spirit unites our spirits with God in such a way that Jesus is always near, and always with us, even though we are on earth and He is in heaven. We can still speak with Him, and He can still hear us. This is why, when speaking about returning to the Father, Jesus still told the disciples that they can still ask Him for things (John 14:14).

What has Jesus been doing since the time of His ascension until now?

Actively Involved

Jesus hasn't abandoned or turned His back on us. Since the time that He returned to heaven until now, He continues to be involved in our activities on earth. It is clear that the apostles believed this because of how they spoke of Him. Peter said it was the power of Jesus' name that healed a man who had been disabled since birth (Acts 3:2-8, 16). Peter also said that Jesus' presence can bring times of refreshing (Acts 3:19), and that Jesus grants forgiveness and gives peace (Acts 5:31, 10:36). He said these things in the present tense, after Jesus has already ascended into heaven. Jesus even appeared to Saul on the road to Damascus after He had ascended to heaven (Acts 9).

Praying for Us

Paul wrote that Jesus prays for us (Rom. 8:34). What does this mean? Prayer is simply talking to God. Jesus, when praying, is talking to the Father. So this means that Jesus is in heaven, talking to the Father about us. Hebrews 7:25 says that Jesus "always lives to make intercession" for those who follow Him. What an amazing thought – to think that the greatest Person in the entire universe, the One who has all authority on heaven and earth, Whose name is greater than any name, is praying for you and me. He cares so deeply about us that He is constantly talking with the Father about us.

Preparing a Place for Us

John 14-16 is a beautiful passage in Scripture where Jesus begins to speak with His disciples about how He must go away. Some portions of this text have already been referenced above, where He speaks about the importance of going away so that He can send the Holy Spirit. Many other amazing and comforting things are said to the disciples as well. For example:

> "In My Father's house are many dwelling places; if it were not so, I would have told you;

> for I go to prepare a place for you. If I go and
> prepare a place for you, I will come again and
> receive you to Myself, that where I am, [there]
> you may be also" (John 14:2-3).

Jesus, while seated in heaven at the right hand of God, while talking with the Father about us, and while being actively involved in the happenings of our lives on earth, is also preparing a place for us. The way Jesus speaks in these verses would have reminded the disciples of traditional Jewish marriage ceremonies. During the betrothal period, the groom would go away to prepare a home for his soon-to-be bride. This would be a very exciting time, where she is waiting expectedly for his return, and he is joyfully preparing everything for her and making it perfect. He has her constantly on his mind, as he prepares for their life together. The bride also never knows exactly when he will return for her, so she keeps herself ready for him at all times. This beautiful symbolism shows how Jesus thinks about us, and how we are to think about His return.

Planning to Return for Us

Jesus said that He will come again to receive those that are His, just as a groom returns to receive the bride after preparing a place for her. No one knows when He will return, but the apostles often spoke about the return, and about their sense that it would be very soon (2 Pet. 3:10; Titus 2:13; Rev. 22:12). The Jewish bride who is waiting for her groom has the sense that he could return at any moment for her, and so she keeps herself pure and ready for him at all times. In the same way, the disciples felt that sense of immediacy. He could return for them at any time, and they wanted to be ready. Jesus said, "Be on the alert, for you do not know which day your Lord is coming...For this reason you also must be ready; for the Son of Man is coming at an hour when you do not think He will" (Matt. 24:42, 44).

It has been around two thousand years since Jesus said He would be coming soon. What is taking Him so long? Has He forgotten about us? On the contrary, it is only by the great patience and goodness of God that Jesus has waited as long as He has. Peter speaks about a "period of restoration of all things" that must come to pass before Jesus returns (Acts 3:20-21). Peter wrote that Jesus is not being lazy by taking as long as He has to return for us. Instead, he is being extremely patient, because He doesn't want any to perish (2 Pet. 3:8-9). You can imagine how excited a groom is to return for his bride. Jesus used this analogy so that we could be certain that He always has us in mind, and that He can't wait much longer to be reunited with us. And yet He waits—not because He is lazy, and not because He doesn't care, but because He is waiting until every single person who will be saved has been saved.

When Jesus returns, it will be great news for some people, and terrible news for others. It will be salvation and life for some people, and it will be eternal punishment for others. Remember, the punishment for sin is death. Those that have not received Jesus' debt forgiveness will experience the fullness of God's wrath. When Jesus returns, He comes as a groom, and also as a judge. He has been appointed to be the "Judge of the living and the dead" (Acts 10:42). Everyone ought to feel the urgency of ensuring that they are restored to God as quickly as possible, because no one knows the exact day of His return.

Advocate

We were legally guilty because of our sin, and Jesus' crucifixion offers us complete debt forgiveness. We were spiritually dead, and Jesus' resurrection offers us life, both now and forever. What about **awaiting judgment**? Does God still remember all those sins that we've done? Even if we were forgiven once, what if we sin again? What happens to those who receive forgiveness and new life and then sin again?

It is true that God hates sin. It is also true that as long as we live in these current bodies of flesh, we will continue to struggle with sin. Paul wrote that we should not continue in sin or let it reign in us (Rom. 6:1, 12), yet he confessed his own continual struggles with sin (Rom. 7:14-25). He also wrote that there is no more condemnation for those that in Christ, despite this continual struggle with sin, and wrote that nothing can separate us from the love of God (Rom. 8:1, 35). Hebrews 4:15 says that Jesus can actually sympathize with our weakness, because He was tempted in every way that we are tempted. He never gave into the temptations or sinned, but He understands the struggle. 1 John 2:1-2 says that if we sin, Jesus is our Advocate with the Father because He paid for those sins.

The wonderful reality is that while Jesus is in heaven, at the right hand of God, talking with the Father about us, part of what they talk about us is our continued struggle with sin. And even though God hates sin, His wrath will not again turn on those who are in Christ because Jesus is advocating for them. He already paid the price for those sins.

God will not inflict wrath upon those who have been forgiven, even if they continue to struggle with sin. Jesus is a constant reminder before the Father that the full price for our sins has been paid. We were awaiting judgment, but now we have an Advocate.

Summary

When Jesus ascended to heaven, He returned to be with the Father. He is still with us in spirit, actively involved in our lives, and concerned about us. He is preparing a place for us, and He will return for us. In the mean time, He is constantly talking with the Father about us, praying for us, and advocating for us while we wait for His return.

Reflection Questions

How long was Jesus on earth, after His resurrection, before His ascension?

Why did Jesus have to return to heaven?

Has Jesus forgotten about us? What is He doing?

What is the significants of Jesus' ascension, in terms of the gospel?

CHAPTER NINE

CONCLUSION

Introduction

The bad news is that we are all sinners, bound for an eternity of punishment in hell. God's justice demands it. Our sinful nature makes us unable to do anything on our own to make it right. The good news is that Jesus Christ came to the earth, died on a cross to pay for our sins, rose from the dead to give us life, is sitting at the right hand of God as our Advocate, and will return to receive those that are His into eternal life with Him. But what do we do with this information? How are we to respond? How can we receive what Jesus is offering?

Three Reactions

When the apostles shared this message with people in the book of Acts, there were essentially three kinds of reactions: Apathy, Anger, or Conviction.

Apathy

Some people simply didn't care enough to take it to heart. When Paul preached in Athens, for example, most of them were simply intrigued, saying things like "We will hear you again on this matter" (Acts 17:32).

Those that hear the gospel and aren't moved to respond to it are in a very dangerous place. Perhaps they think they have more time. They'll reconsider when it's more convenient for them. They remain as they were before: legally guilty, spiritually dead, and awaiting judgment. Since no one knows when they will die, they are taking great risks by procrastinating.

When we truly understand what the gospel message offers us, why would we wait? It would be like winning the lottery and then lazying around for months and months before collecting. We can be restored to God and forgiven of our sins. We can have life, now and forever, instead of death. This can be ours *right now*.

Anger

Some people were angry when they heard the gospel. The message of the gospel is offensive to those that are still dead in their sins. It's not pleasant being confronted with our faults and the reality of the eternal punishment we deserve. Many people, instead of acknowledging their guilt, become angry.

The apostles were often imprisoned, beaten, and forbidden from sharing this message with others. Many of them were killed. The Christian faith has always been persecuted. Even today, in many parts of the world, Christians are being beaten and killed for their faith in Jesus Christ. Jesus is a "stone of stumbling and a rock of offense" (1 Pet. 2:8) to those that are still living in sin. Maybe they don't want to admit that they've done anything wrong. Maybe they don't want to stop the sins that they enjoy. Maybe they don't want anyone telling them what to do.

Whatever the reason, those that hear the gospel and are angered by it, unwilling to acknowledge their sin and their need for salvation, are making a grave mistake. They are giving up eternity. "What will it profit a man if he gains the whole world and forfeits his soul?" (Matt. 16:26).

Conviction

Some people heard the gospel and were convicted. When Peter preached the gospel at Pentecost, those that were convicted were "pierced to the heart, and said, 'Brethren, what shall we do?'" (Acts 2:37).

When you really understand Who God is, what you are, what sin has done, what you deserve, and what Jesus Christ has done to save you, this is the kind of reaction you have. You feel pierced to the heart. You realize you cannot get right with God on your own, and you feel a desperate need for salvation beyond your own means. You cry out, "What can I do to be saved?"

The Call to Action

When Jesus preached the gospel, He called people to respond. Jesus taught the apostles to do the same, so that when they preached, they also called people to respond. Simply hearing the gospel was not enough. There had to be a response, and the proper response was to repent and believe (Acts 3:19, Mark 1:15). What do these words mean?

Repentance is more than just feeling bad. It has to do with changing one's mind or thinking differently than before about something. In terms of the gospel, it means acknowledging sin, admitting guilt, understanding the consequences, and realizing that good behavior can never pay off the debt that is stacked against us because of our sin. It means understanding Who God is, realizing how sin has severed our relationship with Him, and deciding that we don't want to be separated from God anymore. We look at the beauty and glory of God, realize how much more valuable He is than our sinful desires, and we repent of our wickedness.

Belief is more than simply acknowledging Who Jesus is or understanding what He did. We do have to understand the those things and believe that they are true, but belief is more than that. We move from understanding to belief when we decide to put our trust in Jesus for these things. We trust what He said, and what He did. We put our faith in it. We rely on it. We understand that He did *everything* that was necessary for our salvation and that we can do *nothing* to save ourselves, and we rely on Him completely. We put our faith in Jesus, and all that He did, knowing that this faith is what saves us.

> For by grace you have been saved through faith; and that not of yourselves, it is the gift of God; not as a result of works, so that no one may boast (Eph. 2:8-9).

God is not far from any of us (Acts 17:27). He is near, and He doesn't want our sins to separate us from Him any longer. He is our Father, and He wants us to be restored to Him. He has done everything necessary to make that happen. All we have to do is receive it. All we have to do is repent and believe in Jesus Christ, and we can be restored to Him. Isn't it amazing, how simple that is? This is the simplistic beauty of the gospel. What must we do to be saved? Repent and believe.

What Now?

What does life look like after one repents and believes in Jesus Christ? Do we continue to live like we did before? Should we now avoid all of our old friends? Do we need to tell someone about becoming a Christian? Do we need to try and share the gospel with others?

What we see in the book of Acts is that people who believed were united together in this faith. They were a family. They saw each other as brothers and sisters in Christ, and they continued together. We call this church.

> They were continually devoting themselves to the apostles' teaching and to fellowship, to the breaking of bread and to prayer (Acts 2:42)

The Christian is not called to isolation. If you have recently repented and believed in Jesus, your next step should be to find a local church and let them know about it. If someone gave you this book, you should ask them about their church. Many places in the world have many churches within a short distance. Some places in the world have very few churches, and some places have none. A biblical church will receive you with great joy and help you as you explore this new life you have found in Christ. They will love you and help you to grow in your understanding of your faith. They will help you to learn how to read and understand the Bible. They will help you to understand the role of the Holy Spirit in your life, and will give you opportunities to begin to serve.

> Let us hold fast the confession of our hope without wavering, for He who promised is faithful; and let us consider how to stimulate one another to love and good deeds, not forsaking our own assembling together, as is the habit of some, but encouraging [one another;] and all the more as you see the day drawing near (Heb. 10:23-25).

A solid, biblical church will also help you to learn how to walk in this newness of life that you have been given. It's not enough to just say that you believe these truths. You must also begin to walk in them, and a local church and its pastors will help you learn how to do this.

Even though the Bible is very clear that we cannot be saved by good works, it is also very clear that the evidence of real saving faith will be apparent in a changed life. Paul wrote that we cannot save ourselves by good works (Eph. 2:8-9), and yet he also preached that we should perform "deeds appropriate to repentance" (Acts 26:20). When Peter was asked what must be done to be saved, he told them to repent and be baptized (Acts 2:38). James even warned us that faith without works is dead (James 2:26). What do these things mean? Does this mean that we do "deeds appropriate to repentance," be baptized, and have good works in order to be saved? No. These verses emphasize that the evidence of true repentance and faith will be an increasing desire to obey what Jesus commanded. We cannot simply say we believe the gospel and then go on as if nothing has changed. That would be a sign that we didn't ever really repent and believe.

When we truly understand the gospel, when we really repent and put our faith in Jesus Christ, when we are forgiven and given new life, we cannot ever be the same. An inner transformation begins to happen. For some it is immediate and dramatic, and for others it is slow; but it is never missing completely. The more we seek God, the more we will notice that our desires are changing. Our desire for God and the things of God will increase, and our desire for sin will decrease. We will love Him, and want to obey Him, and we will find the fullness of joy in doing so.

Jesus said, "If you love Me, you will keep my commandments" (John 14:15). When He told the apostles to go into all the world and share the gospel, He didn't tell them to simply share the story and move on. He told them to make disciples, and then teach those disciples to obey all that He commanded (Matt. 28:20). So even though we cannot do good works in order to be saved, once we *are* saved, Jesus said that our love for Him will be evidenced by our obedience to what He has commanded.

This is another reason why the local church is so important. They will be able to teach you about what Jesus commanded, and help you to begin to follow Him as a true disciple. They will teach you about many important things, such as baptism, the Lord's Supper, prayer, worship, fellowship, service, and many other things.

Summary

The gospel is powerful in its simplistic beauty. It reveals the glory of God, God's love for man, and the only hope for mankind. I hope that you have felt that power as you have read this book. I hope that this book has given you a better understanding of what the gospel is, that you have believed it, and that your love for God and desire to know Him has increased.

> "This is eternal life, that they may know You, the only true God, and Jesus Christ whom You have sent" (John 17:3).

Reflection Questions

If someone were to ask you to explain the gospel message to them, what would you say?

Has your answer to the above question changed since Chapter 1?

What has been your response to the gospel? Have you believed in Jesus Christ?

Jesus commands His disciples to share the gospel with others Does that make you excited? Concerned? Nervous?

APPENDIX 1

THE TRINITY

Introduction

The word "Trinity" describes the nature of God as seen in the Bible. This doctrine is admittedly difficult to understand, and yet it often comes up when sharing the gospel with people. I decided against including a full explanation of the Trinity in one of the gospel chapters, even though some chapters hinted at it, because the apostles never tried to explain it when sharing the gospel in the book of Acts. The goal of this book was to explain the main elements of the gospel, using the apostles' sermons from the book of Acts as a template.

However, since the Trinity is a very important topic, and since it comes up so frequently when sharing the gospel and talking about the nature of God, I felt it might be helpful to include a brief description here.

The Trinity

The doctrine of the Trinity teaches that there

is one God, and that this God eternally exists as three distinct persons – The Father, the Son, and the Holy Spirit. It does not teach that there are three gods. The Father is God, the Son is God, and the Holy Spirit is God; but there is only one God. It also does not teach that the Father, the Son, and the Holy Spirit are the same person. They are three distinct persons. They are all God. And there is only one God. It is difficult for us to understand how this relationship works, yet this is how the Bible describes God. Here are just a few examples:

Plurality of the Singular

In Genesis 1:26, God said, "Let us make man in our image." Who is God talking to? The next verse says "God created man in His own image." Here God was speaking to Himself, about making man in His own image, and He said "in our image." God was not speaking to angels, for angels did not participate in the creation of men. God alone created everything (Isa. 44:24). So here we have God consulting with Himself, and there is clearly a sense of plurality about His nature.

All are called God

The Father is called God (Gal. 1:3). Jesus is called God (John 1:1, 20:28). The Holy Spirit is called God (Acts 5:3-4). Yet there is only one God. He said "I am the LORD, and there is no other; besides me there is no God" (Isa. 45:5).

Distinction Among the Three

When Jesus is baptized by John the Baptist, Luke wrote that "Holy Spirit descended upon Him in bodily form like a dove, and a voice came out of heaven, 'You are My beloved Son, in You I am well-pleased'" (Luke 3:22). This situation would not have happened if "Father," "Son," and "Holy Spirit" were just different ways to refer to the same person. Jesus said that He will return to the Father, and will send us the Holy Spirit (John 14:2-3, 16:7). Jesus prays to the Father (John 17:1). These are clearly three distinct people, not different ways to refer to the same person.

Summary

The doctrine of the Trinity describes the nature of God, and this nature can be difficult for us to fully grasp. Indeed, there is much about God that is difficult for us to understand. The Bible clearly teaches that there is only one God, that the Father is God, that Jesus is God, that the Holy Spirit is God, and that these three persons are distinct from one another.

In terms of the gospel, the great news is that God the Father sent God the Son to die for our sins. God the Son rose from the dead and ascended back into heaven, and God the Son sent God the Holy Spirit to everyone who believes in Him. Let us not allow things that are difficult to understand keep us from the things that are easy to understand. The gospel is beautiful in its simplicity, and salvation is open to all who will repent and believe in Jesus Christ.

> For God so loved the world, that He gave His only begotten Son, that whoever believes in Him shall not perish, but have eternal life (John 3:16).

> "And we are witnesses of these things; and [so is] the Holy Spirit, whom God has given to those who obey Him" (Acts 5:32).

REFERENCES

Strong, J. 1890a. A *Concise Dictionary of the Words in the Greek Testament; with Their Renderings in the Authorized English Version*. Madison, NC: Abingdon Press, 1890.

————. 1890b. *A concise dictionary of the words in the Hebrew Bible; with their renderings in the Authorized English Version*. Madison, NC: Abingdon Press.

Thayer, J. H., C. L. W. Grimm, and C. G. Wilke. 1889. A Greek-English Lexicon of the New Testament: Being Grimm's Wilke's Clavis Novi Testamenti. Rev. ed. New York, NY: American Book Company.